A Syllabus

of the

History of Chinese Civilization and Culture

SIXTH EDITION

BY

L. C. GOODRICH   H. C. FENN

Illustrated

THE CHINA SOCIETY OF AMERICA, INC., NEW YORK

NOTE TO SIXTH EDITION

This is a revised edition of the Syllabus which appeared successively in 1929, 1934, 1941, 1947, and 1950. The maps and chart prepared by Mr. Fenn have been left unchanged. The text prepared by Mr. Goodrich, however, has been considerably revised and brought up to date.

H. C. F.

L. C. G.

March, 1958.

4

Beginnings of the Chinese People

General reading: Li Chi, The beginnings of Chinese civilization.
Goodrich, L. C.: Archaeology in China: the first decades, JAS 17 (1957), 5-15.

1. Paleolithic man

Woo Ju-k'ang: Human fossils found in China, Scientia Sinica 5 (1956), 389-397.
de Chardin, Early man in China.
................, Fossil men.

2. Neolithic man

Li Chi (ed.), Ch'eng-tzu-yai, the black pottery culture site.
Sekino, T.: On the black pottery of ancient China, MTB 14 (1955), 139-154.
Sommarström, B.: The site of Ma-kia-yao, BMFEA 28 (1956), 55-101.

3. The Hsia period

Creel, Studies in early Chinese culture, 1st ser., 97-131.
Salmony, A.: The problem of pre-Anyang bronzes, Festschrift von der Heydt, 1-7.

4. The Shang period

Creel, The birth of China, 1-37, 57-216.
Cheng Te-k'un: The origin and development of Shang culture, Asia Major, n.s. 6 (1957), 80-98.

II

Historical times: Early Chou

General reading: Creel, The birth of China, 219-380.
Ch'en, Meng-chia: The greatness of Chou (ca. 1027-
ca. 221 B.C.), China (ed. by MacNair), 54-59.
Walker, The multi-state system of ancient China.

1. **The age as seen in earliest literature**

   a. Legge, Chinese classics, IV, 142-171.
   Waley, The book of songs.
   Karlgren, The book of odes.

   b. Karlgren, B.: Glosses on the Book of Documents, BMFEA 20
   (1948), 39-315; 21 (1949), 63-206; 22 (1950), 1-81.
   Mote, F. W.: Review of *Shang-shu shih-i,* JAS 17 (1957), 136-
   140.

   c. Legge, Chinese classics, V, pt. 1, 22-53, 112-135.
   Ch'i, Ssu-ho: Professor Hung on the *Ch'un Ch'iu,* Yenching jo.
   of social studies 1 (1938), 49-71.
   Kennedy, G. A.: Interpretation of the *Ch'un-Ch'iu,* JAOS 62
   (1942), 40-48.

   d. Waley, A.: The book of changes, BMFEA 5 (1933), 121-142.
   Needham and Wang, Science and civilization in China, II, 304-345.

2. **Light thrown on the period by the bronzes**

   Creel, H. G.: Bronze inscriptions of the Western Chou dynasty as
   historical documents, JAOS 56 (1936), 335-349.
   Wenley et al., A descriptive and illustrative catalogue of Chinese
   bronzes.
   Loehr, M.: Ordos daggers and knives, *Artibus Asiae* 12 (1949), 23-83.
   Loehr, Chinese bronze age weapons.
   Karlgren, B.: Yin and Chou in Chinese bronzes, BMFEA 8 (1936),
   9-156.

3. **Language and script**

   Karlgren, The Chinese language, an essay on its nature and history.
   Karlgren, B.: On the script of the Chou dynasty, BMFEA 8 (1936),
   157-178.
   Erkes, E.: The use of writing in ancient China, JAOS 61 (1941),
   127-130.

4. **Legends**

   Karlgren, B.: Legends and cults in ancient China, BMFEA 18 (1946),
   199-365.
   Maspero, H.: La société chinoise à la fin des Chang et au début des
   Tcheou, BEFEO 46, 2 (1954), 335-403.

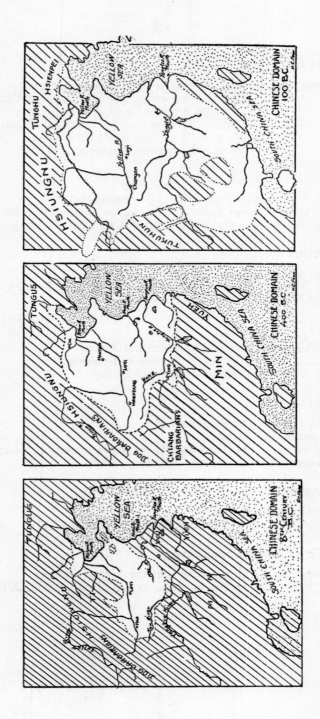

7

Middle and Later Chou

General reading: Wei, The spirit of Chinese culture, chap. 2.
Ch'en, Meng-chia: The greatness of Chou, China
(ed. by MacNair), 59-71.
Lattimore, Inner Asian frontiers of China, chap. 12.
Maspero, La Chine antique, 454-507.
Wittfogel, Oriental despotism, 251-252.

Moulders of thought

Fung, A short history of Chinese philosophy, 1-128.
Liu Wu-chi, A short history of Confucian philosophy, 13-89.
Creel, Chinese thought from Confucius to Mao Tse-tung, 10-114.

a. Confucius

Waley, The analects of Confucius.
Fung, A history of Chinese philosophy (transl. by Bodde), chap. 4.
Creel, Confucius, the man and the myth, 1-172.

b. Mo Ti

Mei, The ethical and political works of Motse.
................, Motse, the neglected rival of Confucius.
Fung, A history of Chinese philosophy, chap. 5.

c. The *Lao-tzu*

Waley, The way and its power.
Duyvendak, Tao te ching.
Creel, H. G.: On two aspects of early Taoism, Silver Jubilee
Volume of . . . Kyoto University, 43-53.

d. Chuang-tzŭ

Fung, Chuang-tzŭ.
Waley, Three ways of thought in ancient China, 17-112.

e. The *Ta hsüeh* and *Chung yung*

Hughes, The Great Learning and the Mean-in-action.
Chan, Wing-tsit: review of above in JAOS 63 (1943), 291-292.

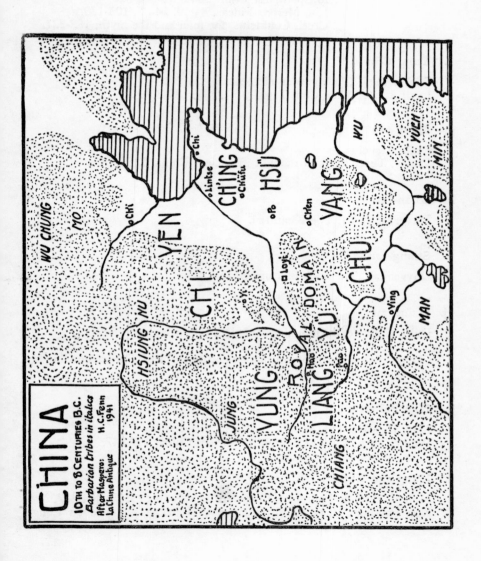

CHINA

10TH TO 8 CENTURIES B.C.
Barbarian tribes in italics   H. C. Fenn
After Maspero: 1941
La Chine Antique

WU CHUNG
MO
Chi
YEN
CHI
HSIUNG NU
JUNG
YUNG
ROYAL DOMAIN
Hsao
Pao
LIANG
CHIANG
YU
Loyi
Yi
Linise
CH'ING
Chüfu
Po
HSÜ
Chen
YANG
CHU
Ying
MAN
WU
MIN
YUEH

9

Moulders of thought, continued

General reading: Fung, The Spirit of Chinese philosophy, 29-58.
Maspero, La Chine antique, 508-580.
Lin, Men and ideas, 44-59, 74-87, 103-120.
Creel, Confucius, the man and the myth, 182-221.

f. Yang Chu

Forke, Yang Chu's garden of pleasure.
Lyall, L. A.: Yang Chu, THM 9 (1939), 189-204.

g. Meng-tzu

Lyall, Mencius.
Waley, Three ways of thought in ancient China, 115-195.

h. Kuan-tzu

Maverick (ed.), The Kuan-tzu.

i. Shang-tzu

Duyvendak, The book of Lord Shang.

j. Hsün-tzu

Dubs, Hsüntze, the moulder of ancient Confucianism.
................., The works of Hsüntze.
Cheng, Hsüntzu's theory of human nature and its influence on Chinese thought.

k. Han Fei-tzu

Liao, Han Fei Tzu, I.
Waley, Three ways of thought in ancient China, 199-247.

l. Kung-sun Lung

Mei, Y. P.: The Kung-sun Lung-tzu, HJAS 16 (1953), 404-437.
Kou Pao-koh, Deux sophistes chinois, Houei et Kong-souen Long.

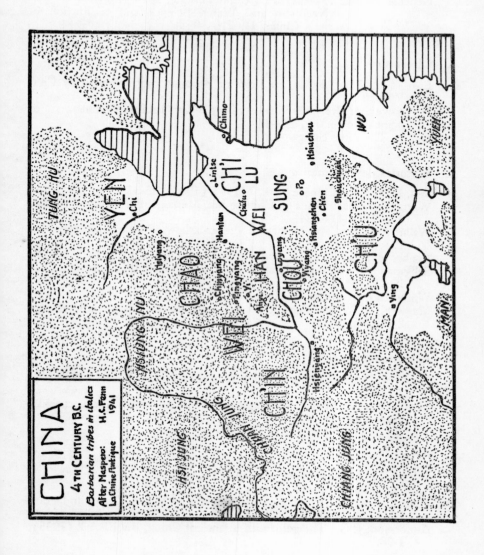

CHINA
4TH CENTURY B.C.
Barbarian tribes in italics
After Maspero: H.C.Fann
La Chine Antique 1941

11

Literature, science, and art in Later Chou

General reading: Maspero, La Chine antique, 581-621.
Needham and Wang, Science and civilization in China, II, 216-246.

1. Literature

Lim (tsl.), The Li Sao, an elegy on encountering sorrows, by Ch'ü Yüan.
Hightower, J. R.: Ch'ü-yüan studies, Silver Jubilee Volume . . . of Kyoto University, 192-223.
Waley, The Nine Songs.

2. Material developments

Wu, K. T.: The Chinese book, THM 3 (1936), 25-33.
Wang, Chi-chen: Notes on Chinese ink, Metropolitan Museum studies 3 (1930), 114-124.
Wilbur, C. M.: The history of the crossbow, Smithsonian rept. for 1936, 427-438.
Loehr, M.: Early knives, Artibus Asiae 14 (1951), 77-162.
Seligman and Beck: Far Eastern glass: some western origins, BMFEA 10 (1938), 1-64.
Wang, Early Chinese coinage.
Maglioni, R.: Archeology in south China, Jo. of East Asiatic studies 2 (1952), 1-20.

3. Astronomy

Maspero, H.: L'astronomie chinoise avant les Han, TP 26 (1928-29), 267-356.
Chatley, H.: Ancient Chinese astronomy, Royal astron. soc. occasional notes 5 (1939), 65-74.

4. Art

White, Tomb tile pictures of ancient China.
................, Tombs of old Lo-yang.
Hochstadter, W.: Pottery and stonewares of Shang, Chou, and Han, BMFEA 24 (1952), 81-108.
Andersson, J. G.: The goldsmith in ancient China, BMFEA 7 (1935), 1-38.

VI

The beginning of empire

General reading: Latourette, The Chinese their history and culture, I, 88-119.
Hudson, Europe and China, chap. 2.

1. **The Ch'in dynasty**

Bodde, China's first unifier.
................., Statesman, patriot, and general.

2. **Relations with the Hsiung-nu and other tribes**

Jettmar, K.: The Altai before the Turks, BMFEA 23 (1951), 135-223.
Lattimore, Inner Asian frontiers of China, 379-390, 399-425, 523-529.

3. **The founding of the Han**

Dubs, H. H.: Han Kao-tsu and Hsiang-yü, JNCBRAS 67 (1936), 58-80.
Dubs (tsl.), The history of the former Han dynasty, by Pan Ku, I.
DeFrancis, J.: Biography of the marquis of Huai-yin, HJAS 10 (1947), 179-215.

4. **The government and code of the Han**

Wang, Yü-ch'üan: An outline of the central government of the Han dynasty, HJAS 12 (1949), 134-187.
Houn, F. W.: The civil service recruitment system of the Han dynasty, Tsing Hua Jo. of Chinese studies, n.s. 1 (1956), 138-164.
Hulsewé, Remnants of Han law.

5. **Expansion of the empire**

Hirth, F.: The story of Chang K'ien, China's pioneer in western Asia, JAOS 37 (1917), 89-152.
Dubs, A Roman city in ancient China.
Aurousseau, L.: La première conquête chinoise des pays annamites, BEFEO 23 (1923), 137-264.
Sansom, G. B.: An outline of recent Japanese archaeological research in Korea, Trans. of the Asiatic Soc. of Japan, 2nd ser., 6 (1929), 5-19.

6. **Impact upon the west**

Teggart, Rome and China.
Shiratori, K.: The geography of the Western Region studied on the basis of the Ta-ch'in accounts, MTB 15 (1956), 73-163.
Laufer, Sino-Iranica, 190-191, 208-213, 221-228, 535-541.

The Former Han dynasty

General reading: Goodrich, A short history of the Chinese people, 36-43.

Dubs (tsl.), The history of the former Han dynasty, II.

1. Economic conditions

Swann, Food and money in ancient China, *Han shu* 24.

Blue, R.: The argumentation of the *Shih-huo chih,* HJAS 11 (1948), 1-70.

Gale (tsl.), Discourses on salt and iron.

Gale, Lin, and Boodberg (tsl.): Discourses on salt and iron, JNCBRAS 65 (1934), 73-110.

Wilbur, Slavery in China during the Former Han dynasty.

2. The first historian: Ssu-ma Ch'ien

Chavannes, Les mémoires historiques de Se-ma Ts'ien, I, xxv-xlvi, clxxxvi, ccxxii-ccxxv, ccxxxiv-ccxli.

Watson, Ssu-ma Ch'ien: Grand historian of China.

3. Confucianism and native cults

Dubs, H. H.: The victory of Han Confucianism, JAOS 58 (1938), 435-449.

Creel, Confucius, the man and the myth, 222-248.

Dubs, H. H.: An ancient Chinese mystery cult, Harvard theol. review 35 (1945), 221-240.

Bielenstein, H.: An interpretation of the portents of the *Ts'ien Han shu,* BMFEA 22 (1950), 127-143.

4. Science

Needham and Wang, Science and civilization in China, I, 109-112; II, 247-303.

Maspero, H.: Les instruments astronomiques des chinois aux temps des Han, MCB 6 (1938-1939), 183-370.

Dubs, H. H.: Solar eclipses during the former Han, Osiris 5 (1938), 499-522.

5. Wang Mang

Dubs, History of the Former Han dynasty, III.

Bielenstein, H.: The restoration of the Han dynasty, BMFEA 26 (1954), 1-210.

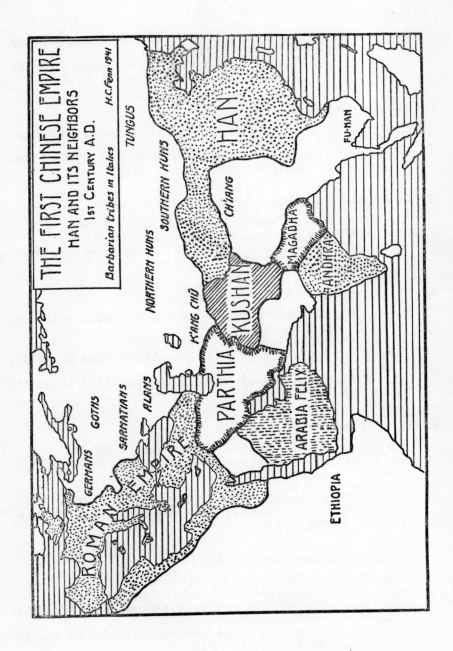

THE FIRST CHINESE EMPIRE
HAN AND ITS NEIGHBORS
1st CENTURY A.D.

Barbarian tribes in Italics   H.C.Fenn 1941

TUNGUS

HAN

FU-NAN

SOUTHERN HUNS

NORTHERN HUNS

CHIANG

MAGADHA

KUSHAN

ANDHRA

K'ANG CHÜ

ALANS

SARMATIANS

PARTHIA

GOTHS

GERMANS

ARABIA FELIX

ROMAN EMPIRE

ETHIOPIA

15

The Later Han dynasty

    General reading: Waley, A.: Life under the Han dynasty, History
        today, 3 (1953), 89-98.
        Maspero, H.: La vie courante dans la Chine des
        Han, Mélanges posthumes, III, 65-76.

1. Military conquests

Chavannes, E.: Trois généraux chinois de la dynastie des orientaux,
    TP 7 (1906), 210-269.
Maspero, H.: L'expedition de Ma Yüan, BEFEO 18 (1918), 11-28.
Stein, R. A.: Le Lin-yi, Han-hiue 2 (1947), 1-335.

2. Taoism and alchemy

Creel, H. G.: What is Taoism? JAOS 76 (1956), 139-152.
Dubs, H. H.: The beginnings of alchemy, Isis 38 (1947), 62-75.
Levy, H. S.: Yellow Turban religion and rebellion at the end of Han,
    JAOS 76 (1956), 214-224.

3. The entrance of Buddhism

Maspero, H.: Les origines de la communauté bouddhiste de Loyang,
    JA 225 (1934), 87-107.
Bagchi, Le canon bouddhique en Chine, I, 3-71.
Edwards, R.: The cave reliefs at Ma Hao, Artibus Asiae 17 (1954),
    5-129.
Lao Kan: Six-tusked elephants on a Han bas-relief, HJAS 17 (1954),
    366-369.

4. Thought and scholarship

Galt, History of Chinese educational institutions, I, 187-269.
Tjan, Po hu t'ung. The comprehensive discussions in the White Tiger
    Hall.
Forke, Lun hêng, I, II.
Li Shi-yi: Wang Ch'ung, THM 5 (1937), 162-184, 290-307.
Balazs, E.: Le crise sociale et la philosophie politique à la fin des Han,
    TP 39 (1949), 83-131.

5. The historians: Pan Piao, Pan Ku, Pan Chao

Swann, Pan Chao, the foremost woman scholar of China.
Sargent, C.: Subsidized history, FEQ 3 (1944), 119-143.
Dubs, H. H.: The reliability of Chinese histories, FEQ 6 (1946),
    23-43.
Franke, H.: Some remarks on the interpretation of Chinese dynastic
    histories, Oriens 3 (1950), 113-122.

5. Economic conditions and trade

Chi, Key economic areas in Chinese history, 113-130.
Blue, R.: The argumentation of the *Shih-huo chih*, HJAS 11 (1948) 76-89.
Kato, S.: On the hang or the associations of merchants in China, MTB 8 (1936), 45-83.
Balazs, S.: Beiträge zur Wirtschafts-geschichte der T'ang-Zeit, MSOS, 34-36 (1931-1933).
Reischauer, E. O.: Notes on T'ang dynasty sea routes, HJAS 5 (1940), 142-164.
Pelliot, P.: Deux itinéraires de Chine en Inde à la fin du VIIIe siècle, BEFEO 4 (1904), 131-413.
Laufer, Sino-Iranica, 488-528, 541-543.
Twitchett, D. C.: The salt commissioners after An Lu-shan's rebellion, AM n.s. 4 (1954), 60-89.
............: Monastic estates in T'ang China, AM n.s. 5 (1956), 123-146.

6. Administration under the T'ang

Rotours, Traité des fonctionnaires et traité de l'armée, traduits de la Nouvelle Histoire des T'ang.
............, Le traité des examens traduit de la Nouvelle Histoire des T'ang.
Bünger, K.: Quellen zur rechtgeschichte der T'ang-zeit.
Rideout, J. K.: The rise of the eunuchs during the T'ang dynasty, AM n.s. 1 (1949), 53-74; 3 (1952), 42-58.
Twitchett, D. C.: The fragments of the T'ang Ordinances of the Department of Waterways discovered at Tun-Huang, AM n.s. 6 (1957), 23-79.

23

XIV

The arts under the Sui and T'ang

General reading: Waley, An introduction to the study of Chinese painting, chap. 8.

1. Poetry

Waley, Translations from the Chinese, 108-298.
................, Life and times of Po Chü-i.
................, The poetry and career of Li Po, 701-762.
Hung, Tu Fu, China's greatest poet.

2. Prose

Edwards, Chinese prose literature of the T'ang period.
Giles, Gems of Chinese literature, 113-130.
Wang, Traditional Chinese tales.
Margouliès, Le kou-wen chinois, lxxii-lxxix, 176-219.
................, Anthologie raisonnée de la littérature Chinoise, 75-81.

3. Sculpture

Sirén, Chinese sculpture from the 5th to 14th centuries, I, 86-114.
Hentze, Chinese tomb figures, 59-114.
Sickman and Soper, The art and architecture of China, 53-62, 70-77.

4. Painting and architecture

Sickman and Soper, *op. cit.,* 78-102, 236-254.
Soper, A.: The famous painters of the T'ang dynasty, Archives of the Chinese Art Society of America, 4 (1950), 7-28.
Acker, Some T'ang and pre-T'ang texts on Chinese painting.

5. Gold, silver, porcelain

Gyllensvärd, Bo: T'ang gold and silver, BMFEA 29 (1957), 1-230.
Lindberg, G.: Hsing-yao and ting-yao, BMFEA 25 (1953), 19-32.

6. The invention of block printing

Carter and Goodrich, The invention of printing in China and its spread westward, 31-66.
Giles, Six centuries at Tunhuang, 43-46.

The Five Dynasties, Liao, Sung, and Chin

General reading: Latourette, The Chinese their history and culture, I, 222-261.
Goodrich, A short history of the Chinese people, 139-166.

1. Military anarchy at the close of T'ang

Levy, Biography of Huang Ch'ao.
Eberhard, Conquerors and rulers, social forces in mediaeval China, 52-64, 89-121.
Schafer, The empire of Min.
――――――, The history of the empire of Southern Han, in Silver Jubilee Vol. of . . . Kyoto Univ., 339-369.

2. The Ch'i-tan (Liao dynasty)

Wittfogel and Fêng, History of Chinese society, Liao (907-1125).
Fêng, C. S.: The Ch'i-tan script, JAOS 68 (1948), 14-18.
Torii, Sculptured stone tombs of the Liao dynasty.
Tamura, J. and Kobayashi, Y.: Tombs and mural paintings of Ch'ing-ling, Japan Qu. 1 (1954), 34-45.

3. The Jurchen (Chin dynasty)

Grousset, Histoire de l'extrême-orient, I, 188-194.
Chavannes, E.: Voyageurs chinois chez les Khitan et les Joutchen, JA, 9 ser., 11 (1898), 361-439.

4. Wang An-shih and his reforms

Williamson, Wang An Shih.
Lin, Men and ideas, chap. 11.

5. Trade with foreign lands

Hirth and Rockhill, Chau Ju-kuo: his work on the Chinese and Arab trade in the 12th and 13th centuries, entitled Chu-fan-chï.
Lo, Jung-pang: China as a sea power, FEQ 14 (1955), 489-503.
Kuwabara, J.: On P'u Shou-keng, MTB 2 (1928), 17-79; 7 (1935), 1-104.
Minorsky, Marvazi on China.
Chou, Yi-liang: Notes on Marvazi's account on China, HJAS 9 (1945), 13-23.

XVI

The civilization of the Sung

General reading: Waley, An introduction to Chinese painting, 179,
203-204, 215-234.
Kracke, E. A., Jr.: Sung society, change within
tradition, FEQ 14 (1955), 479-488.

1. Prose and poetry

Giles, History of Chinese literature, 209-243.
Lin Yutang, The Gay Genius: the life and times of Su Tungpo.
Candlin, The herald wind.
................, The rapier of Lu.

2. Fiction and drama

Prüsek, J.: Story telling in the Sung period, Archiv Orientalni 11
(1939-40), 23 (1955).
................: The narrators of Buddhist scriptures and religious tales
in the Sung period, *ibid.* 10 (1938), 375-389.
Erkes, E.: Das chinesische theater vor der T'ang-zeit von Wang
Kuo-wei, AM 10 (1935), 229-246.

3. Philosophy

Fung, A history of Chinese philosophy, II, 408-592.
Bruce, Chu Hsi and his masters.
Huang, Lu Hsiang-shan, a twelfth century Chinese idealist phi-
losopher.
de Bary, W. T.: A reappraisal of Neo-Confucianism, in Wright (ed.),
Studies in Chinese Thought, 81-111.

4. Painting and porcelain

Sirén, A history of early Chinese painting, I, 121-138; II, 1-115.
Sakanishi (tsl.), An essay on landscape painting by Kuo Hsi.
Soper, A. C.: A Northern Sung descriptive catalogue of paintings,
JAOS 69 (1949), 18-33.
................, Kuo Jo-hsü's experiences in painting.
Sickman and Soper, The art and architecture of China, 94-145.
Hobson, A catalogue of Chinese pottery and porcelain in the collection
of Sir Percival David.
Lindberg, G.: Hsing-yao and Ting-yao, BMFEA 25 (1953), 33-71.

5. Architecture

Sickman and Soper, *op. cit.,* 255-282.
Soper, A. C.: Hsiang-kuo-ssŭ, an important temple of northern Sung,
JAOS 68 (1948), 19-45.
Ito, Architectural decoration in China, I, 74-87.

The Sung, continued

General reading : Elisseeff, V. (ed.), L'art de la Chine des Song, 8-24.

1. Music

Courant, M. : Essai historique sur la musique classique des Chinois, Encyclopédie de la musique, I, 77-208.
Sachs, The rise of music in the ancient world, east and west, 105-153.
Levis, Foundations of Chinese musical art.
Hartner, W. : Some notes on Chinese musical art, Isis 78 (1938), 72-94.

2. Gardens

Sirén, Gardens of China, chaps. 1-5.
Tung, C. : Chinese gardens, THM 3 (1936), 220-244.
Huc, A journey through the Chinese empire, I, 202-207.

3. Mathematics

Mikami, The development of mathematics in China and Japan, 56-88.
Konantz, E. L. : The precious mirror of the four elements, China jo. 2 (1924), 304-310.
Vanhée, L. : Li Yé, mathématicien chinois de XIIIe siècle, TP 14 (1913), 537-568.

4. The Jewish colony at K'aifeng

White, Chinese Jews.
Tobar, Inscriptions juives de K'ai-fong.
Löwenthal, R. : The nomenclature of the Jews in China, MS 12 (1947), 97-126.
.... : The Jews in China, an annotated bibliography, CSPSR 24 (1940), 113-234.
.... : The early Jews in China : a supplementary bibliography, Folklore studies 5 (1946), 353-398.

5. Plant introductions

Goodrich, L. C. : Cotton in China, Isis 97 (1943), 408-410.
Hagerty, M. J. : Comments on writings concerning Chinese sorghums, HJAS 5 (1941), 234-260.
Ho Ping-ti : Early ripening rice in Chinese history, Econ. hist. review, 2nd ser., 9 (1956), 200-218.

6. Examinations for government office

Kracke, E. A., Jr. : Family vs. merit in Chinese civil service examinations under the empire, HJAS 10 (1947), 103-123.
.... , Civil service in early Sung China, 960-1067.
.... : Region, family, and individual in the Chinese examination system, in Fairbank (ed.), Chinese Thought and Institutions, 251-268.

The Mongol empire in eastern Asia

General reading: Latourette, The Chinese their history and culture, I, 262-282.

1. **The conquest of China**

Martin, The rise of Chinghis Khan and his conquest of North China.
Grousset, L'empire des steppes, 286-293, 308-309, 321-324, 349-356.

2. **The expeditions to Japan, Indo-China, and Java**

Sansom, Japan, a short cultural history, 309-321.
Grousset, *op. cit.,* 356-359.
Groenveldt, W. P.: The expedition of the Mongols against Java in 1293 A.D., China rev. 4 (1875-1876), 246-254.
Pelliot, Mémoires sur les coutumes du Cambodge de Tcheou Ta-Kouan, version nouvelle, 99-119.

3. **Travellers to and from China**

Olschki, Marco Polo's precursors.
................, Guillaume Boucher.
Moule and Pelliot, Marco Polo, the descriptions of the world.
Moule, Quinsai, with other notes on Marco Polo.
Waley, Ch'ang-ch'un, the travels of an alchemist.
Bretschneider, Mediaeval researches from eastern Asiatic sources, 3-24, 109-172.
Moule, Christians in China: before the year 1550, chap. 4.

4. **Economic conditions**

Schurmann, Economic structure of the Yüan dynasty.
Rockhill, W. W.: Notes on the relations and trade of China with the eastern archipelago and the coast of the Indian Ocean during the 14th century, TP 14 (1913), 473-476; 15 (1914), 419-447.
Franke, Geld und Wirtschaft in China unter der Mongolen-Herrschaft.

5. **Nestorians and Catholics**

Moule, *op. cit.,* 145-264.
Dawson, The Mongol mission, Narratives and letters of Franciscan missionaries.
Rouleau, F. A.: The Yangchow Latin tombstone, HJAS 17 (1954), 346-365.
Foster, J.: Crosses from the walls of Zaitun, JRAS (1954), 1-25.
Bernard, La découverte de Nestoriens Mongols aux Ordos et l'histoire ancienne du Christianisme en extrême-orient.

6. **Taoism and Buddhism**

Ten Broeck, J. R. and Yiu Tung: A Taoist inscription of the Yüan dynasty, TP 40 (1950), 60-122.
Chavannes, E.: Inscriptions et pièces de chancellerie chinoises de l'époque mongole, TP 5 (1904), 366-447; 6 (1905), 1-42.

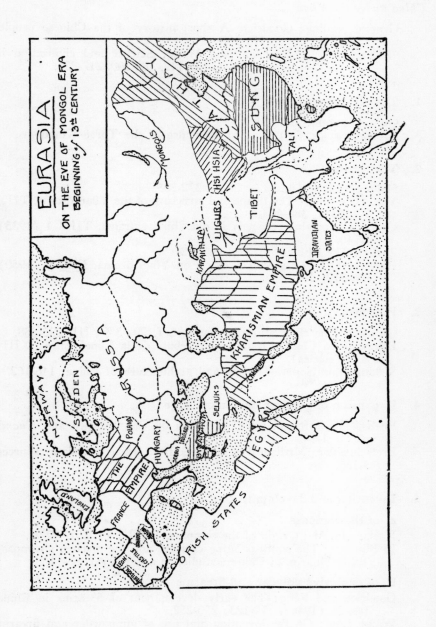

31

China under the Yüan

General reading: Goodrich, A short history of the Chinese people,
171-188.
Needham and Wang, Science and civilization in
China, I, 140-142, 188-190, 217-221.

1. **The picaresque tale**

Ou, Le roman chinois, 21, 31-40, 52-61.
Brewitt-Taylor, San Kuo, or Romance of the Three Kingdoms.

2. **The theatre**

Hsiung, Shih-i: Drama in China, 372-385.
Yao, Hsin-nung: The theme and structure of the Yüan drama, THM
1 (1935), 388-403.
Ch'ien, Chung-shu: Tragedy in old Chinese drama, THM 1 (1935),
37-46.
Zucker, The Chinese theater, chap. 2.
Hightower, J. R.: a review article on Yüan drama, FEQ 9 (1950),
208-212.

3. **Fine arts**

Grousset, The civilizations of the east, I, 291-339; III, 333-338.
Pouzyna, La Chine, l'Italie et les débuts de la Renaissance (XIIIe-
XIVe siècles).
Sickman and Soper, The art and architecture of China, 146-162.

4. **Expansion of geographical knowledge**

Fuchs, The "Mongol atlas" of China by Chu Ssu-pen and *Kuang-
yü-t'u,* 1-14.
Bretschneider, Mediaeval researches from eastern Asiatic sources,
3-136.

5. **Invention and development**

a. **of the compass**
Hashimoto, M.: Origin of the compass, MTB 1 (1926), 69-92.
Li Shu-hua: The south-pointing carriage and the mariner's compass,
Tsing Hua jo. of Chinese studies, n.s. 1 (1956), 63-113.

b. **of explosive powder and firearms**
Goodrich and Fêng: The early development of firearms in China,
Isis 36 (1946), 114-123; 250-252.
Wang, Ling: On the invention and use of gunpowder and firearms
in China, Isis 37 (1947), 160-178.

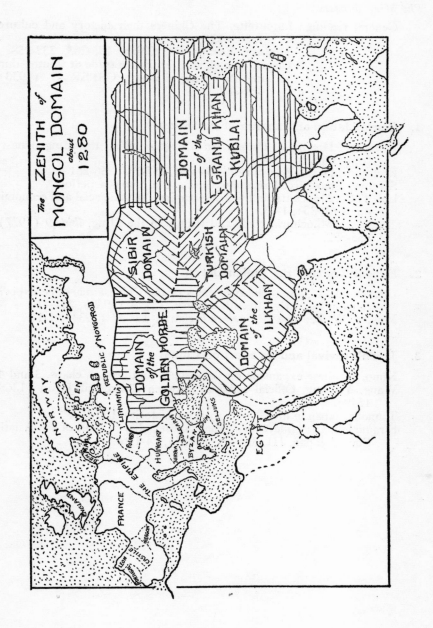

The ZENITH of MONGOL DOMAIN about 1280

DOMAIN of the GRAND KHAN KUBLAI

SIBIR DOMAIN

TURKISH DOMAIN

DOMAIN of the ILKHAN

DOMAIN of the GOLDEN HORDE

REPUBLIC of NOVGOROD

NORWAY

SWEDEN

DENMARK

LITHUANIA

THE EMPIRE

FRANCE

HUNGARY

SERVIA

BULGARIA

BYZAN'

SELJUKS

EGYPT

CASTILE

LEON

PORTUGAL

ENGLAND

SCOTLAND

The Ming dynasty

General reading: Latourette, The Chinese their history and culture, I, 283-308.

Hudson, Europe and China, 195-203, 232-258.

Chang, Teh-ch'ang: Maritime trade at Canton during the Ming dynasty, CSPSR 17 (1933), 264-282

1. Consolidation and territorial expansion

Pokotilov, History of the eastern Mongols during the Ming dynasty from 1368 to 1634.

Bretschneider, Mediaeval researches, II, 157-167, 256-261.

Serruys, Sino-Jürčed relations during the Yung-lo period.

Lin, T. C.: Manchuria in the Ming empire, Nankai social and economic qu. 8 (1935), 1-43.

.................: Manchuria trade and tribute in the Ming, *ibid.* 9 (1937), 855-892.

2. Expeditions into the Indian Ocean

Duyvendak, J. J. L.: The true dates of the Chinese maritime expeditions in the early fifteenth century, TP 34 (1939), 341-412.

Mulder, W. Z.: The *Wu pei chih* charts, TP 37 (1934), 1-14.

3. Japan's revival and its effect on China

Kuno, Japanese expansion on the Asiatic continent, I, chaps. 3 and 4.

Wang, Yi-t'ung, Official relations between China and Japan (1368-1549).

Tsunoda, Japan in the Chinese dynastic histories, 106-161.

Stramigioli, G.: Hideyoshi's expansionist policy, Trans. of the Asiatic Soc. of Japan, III, 3rd ser. (1954), 74-116.

4. European contacts

a. Portuguese and Spanish

Kammerer, La découverte de la Chine par les Portugais au XVIe siècle.

Chang, Sino-Portuguese trade from 1514 to 1644.

Pelliot, P.: Un ouvrage sur les premiers temps de Macao, TP 31 (1934), 58-94.

Boxer, Fidalgos in the Far East, 1550-1770.

—————, South China in the sixteenth century.

Schurz, The Manila galleon, 1-98.

Laufer, B.: The relations of the Chinese to the Philippine Islands, Smithsonian Inst. misc. collections, 50 (1907), 248-281.

b. Dutch and British

Morse, The chronicles of the East India Company trading to China, I, 1-13.

c. Russia

Pavlovsky, Chinese-Russian relations.

Liu, Hsüan-min: Russo-Chinese relations up to the treaty of Nerchinsk, CSPSR 23 (1940), 391-440.

d. Roman Catholic missionaries

Rowbotham, Missionary and mandarin, the Jesuits at the court of China, 37-78.

Gallagher (tsl.), China in the 16th century: the journals of Matthew Ricci: 1583-1610.

Culture under the Ming

General reading: Goodrich, A short history of the Chinese people, chap. 7.
Needham and Wang, Science and civilization in China, I, 143-149.

1. **Porcelain and lacquer**

Pope, Chinese porcelains from the Ardebil shrine.
Hobson, The wares of the Ming.
Low-Beer, F.: Chinese lacquer of the early 15th century, BMFEA 22 (1950), 145-167.
Jansé, O. R. T.: Notes on Chinese influences in the Philippines in pre-Spanish times, HJAS 8 (1944), 34-62.

2. **Painting and architecture**

Sirén, History of later Chinese painting.
Dubosc, J. P.: A new approach to Chinese painting, Oriental art 3 (1950), 3-10.
Prip-Møller, Chinese Buddhist monasteries.
Sickman and Soper, The art and architecture of China, 163-187, 283-288.

3. **Drama**

Zucker, The Chinese theater, chap. 3.
Yao, Hsin-nung: The rise and fall of the K'un Ch'ü, THM 2 (1936), 63-84.
.... (tsl.): Madame Cassia, THM 1 (1935), 540-584.
Hsiung (tsl.): The romance of the western chamber.
.... (tsl.): Lady Precious Stream.

4. **Fiction**

Irwin, The evolution of a Chinese novel: Shui-hu-chuan.
Bishop, The colloquial short story in China.
Kao, Chinese wit and humor, 62-148.

5. **Wang Yang-ming**

Henke, The philosophy of Wang Yang-ming.
Wang, La philosophe morale de Wang Yang-ming.

6. **Chinese scholarship and thought control**

Busch, H.: The Tung-lin shu-yüan and its political and philosophical significance, MS 14 (1955), 1-163.
Hucker, C. O.: The Tung-lin movement of the later Ming period, in Fairbank (ed.), Chinese thought and institutions, 132-162.
Wu, K. T.: Ming printing and printers, HJAS 7 (1943), 203-260.
Hummel (ed.), Eminent Chinese of the Ch'ing period, *sub* Hsü Kuang-ch'i, Hsü Hung-tsu, Sun Ch'i-fêng, Chu Chih-yü, and Huang Tsung-hsi.
Goodrich, L. C. (tsl.): A study of literary persecution during the Ming, by Ku Chieh-kang, HJAS 3 (1939), 254-311.

The Manchus and their empire

General reading: Fitzgerald, China, chaps. 27-28.
    Fuchs, W.: The personal chronicle of the first
    Manchu emperor, PA 9 (1936), 78-85.

1. **Origin and consolidation of power in Manchuria**

Michael, The origin of Manchu rule in China.
Lattimore, Inner Asian frontiers of China, 103-138.
Li, Chi: Manchuria in history, CSPSR 16 (1932), 226-259.

2. **Collapse of the Ming**

Maspero, H.: Preface to Backhouse and Bland, Les empereurs mand-
    chous, trans. by L. M. Mitchell, 7-24.
Hummel (ed.), Eminent Chinese of the Ch'ing period, *sub* Li Tzu-
    ch'êng, Chang Hsien-chung, Chu Yu-chiao, Chu Yu-chien, Chu
    Yu-lang, Chêng Ch'êng-kung.
Parsons, J. B.: The culmination of a Chinese peasant rebellion: Chang
    Hsien-chung in Szechwan, 1644-46, JAS 16 (1957), 387-400.

3. **Territorial expansion**

Grousset, Histoire de l'extrême-orient, II, 526-542.

4. **Manchu literature and language**

Möllendorff, P. G. von: Essay on Manchu literature, JNCBRAS 24
    (1889-1890), 1-45.
Fuchs, Beiträge zur Mandjurischen bibliographie und literatur.
Fuchs, W.: Neue beiträge zur Mandjurischen bibliographie und
    literatur, MS 7 (1942), 1-37.

5. **Laws and administration**

Staunton, Ta Tsing Leu Lee.
Hsieh, The government of China, 1644-1911.
Fairbank, J. K. and Têng, S. Y.: [Studies of administration under the
    Ch'ing], HJAS 4 (1939), 5 (1940), 6 (1941).
Lu, Les greniers publics de prévoyance sous le dynastie des Ts'ing.
Li, Les censeurs sous la dynastie mandchoue (1616-1911) en Chine.

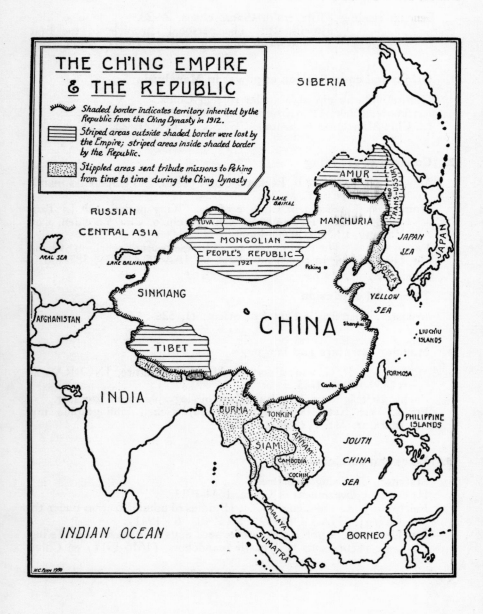

THE CH'ING EMPIRE
& THE REPUBLIC

Shaded border indicates territory inherited by the
Republic from the Ch'ing Dynasty in 1912.

Striped areas outside shaded border were lost by
the Empire; striped areas inside shaded border
by the Republic.

Stippled areas sent tribute missions to Peking
from time to time during the Ch'ing Dynasty.

SIBERIA

RUSSIAN

CENTRAL ASIA

ARAL SEA

LAKE BALKASH

LAKE BAIKAL

TUVA

MONGOLIAN
PEOPLE'S REPUBLIC
1921

MANCHURIA

AMUR

TRANS-USSURI

JAPAN

SINKIANG

Peking

KOREA

JAPAN
SEA

AFGHANISTAN

TIBET

NEPAL

CHINA

Shanghai

YELLOW
SEA

LIU CHIU
ISLANDS

INDIA

Canton

FORMOSA

BURMA

TONKIN

ANNAM

SIAM

CAMBODIA

COCHIN

SOUTH

CHINA

SEA

PHILIPPINE
ISLANDS

INDIAN OCEAN

MALAYA

SUMATRA

BORNEO

H.C.Pinn 1950

38

Chinese culture during the Ch'ing

General reading: Goodrich, A short history of the Chinese people, chap. 8.

1. Literature

Ou, Le roman chinois, 23-26, 63-78, 141-150.
Wang (tsl.), Dream of the red chamber.
Ho (tsl.), Jou lin wai che, le roman des lettrés.
Lin Yutang (tsl.): Six chapters of a floating life, THM 1 (Aug.-Nov. 1935).
Waley, Yuan Mei, eighteenth century Chinese poet.
Giles (tsl.), Strange stories from a Chinese studio.
Lin (tsl.), The nun of T'ai-shan.

2. Drama

Zucker, The Chinese theater, chap. 4.
Arlington and Acton (tsl. and ed.), Famous Chinese plays.
Yao Hsin-nung (tsl.): The right to kill, THM 2 (1936), 468-507.

3. The *Ssu k'u ch'üan shu,* and efforts at thought control

Goodrich, L. C.: China's greatest book, PA 7 (1934), 62-70.
Hung, W.: Preface to an index to *Ssu-k'u ch'üan-shu tsung-mu* and *Wei-shou shu-mu,* HJAS 4 (1939), 47-58.
Goodrich, The literary inquisition of Ch'ien-lung.

4. Thought and historical criticism

Hu, Shih: The Chinese renaissance, China Year Book (1924), 633-637.
Freeman, M.: [17th-18th century thinkers], JNCBRAS 57 (1926); 59 (1928); 64 (1933).
Lin, Men and ideas, chaps. 13-14.
Hummel (ed.): Eminent Chinese of the Ch'ing period, *sub* Huang Tsung-hsi, Ku Yen-wu, Li Yung, Yen Jo-chü, Tai Chen, et al.

5. The literary examinations

Li, L'examen provincial en Chine . . . sous la dynastie des Ts'ing.
Zi, Pratique des examens littéraires en Chine.
Têng, Ssu-yü: Chinese influence on the western examination system, HJAS 7 (1943), 267-312.
Hsü, Francis L. K.: Social mobility in China, American Sociological Review, XIV (1949), 764-771.

6. Imperial and private gardens

Malone, History of the Peking summer palaces under the Ch'ing dynasty.
Sekino and Takeshima, Jehol.
Sirén, Gardens of China.

The Ch'ing dynasty, continued

General reading: Li, The political history of China, 1840-1928, 1-244.
Fairbank, The United States and China, 120-173.
Têng and Fairbank, China's response to the West.

1. Relations with Europe

Morse and MacNair, Far Eastern international relations, chaps. 4-15, 18-23.
Kuo, A critical study of the first Anglo-Chinese war, with documents.
Fox, British admirals and Chinese pirates, 1832-1869.
Têng, Chang Hsi and the treaty of Nanking, 1842.
Sun, Chinese railways and British interests, 1898-1911.

2. Relations with the United States

Dennett, Americans in Eastern Asia.
Swisher, China's management of the American barbarians.

3. Relations with neighboring states

Hsü, China and her political entity.
Rockhill, China's intercourse with Korea from the XVth century to 1895.
Petech, China and Tibet in the early 18th century.
Li, The historical status of Tibet, chaps. 3-4.
Devéria, Histoire des relations de la Chine avec l'Annam-Vietnam du XVIᵉ au XIXᵉ siècle, d'après des documents chinois.

4. Imperial disintegration

a. The Moslem rebellions
Broomhall, Islam in China, 129-163.
✓ Fairbank and Wright (eds.): Documentary collections on modern Chinese history, JAS 17 (1957), 80-86.

b. The Taiping rebellion
Hail, Tsêng Kuo-fan and the Tai Ping rebellion.
Bales, Tso Tsung-t'ang.
Fairbank and Wright (eds.): *op. cit.* 67-76.

c. The Nien rebellion
Chiang, The Nien rebellion.
Fairbank and Wright (eds.): *op. cit.* 76-80.

d. The Boxer uprising
Tan, the Boxer catastrophe.
Fairbank and Wright (eds.): *op. cit.* 105-109.

5. The Reform movement

Hsiao, Kung-chuan: Weng T'ung-ho and the reform movement of 1898, Tsing Hua jo. of Chinese studies, I n.s. (1957), 111-243.
Fairbank and Wright (eds.): *op. cit.* 99-105.
Wright, The T'ung-chih restoration.

Non-political exchanges with the West

General reading: Hughes, The invasion of China by the western world, 1-132.

1. The effect of China's culture

a. on Europe

Reichwein, China and Europe.
Maverick, China, a model for Europe.
Lach, Contributions of China to German civilization, 1648-1740.
Appleton, A cycle of Cathay.
Creel, Confucius, the man and the myth, 254-285.

b. on the Americas

Schurz, The Manila galleon, introduction.
Greenbie, Gold of Ophir, the China trade in the making of America.
Danton, The culture contacts of the United States and China, 1784-1844.
Swingle, W. T.: Our agricultural debt to Asia, in The Asian legacy and American life, 84-103.

2. The effect of Western science on China

Peake, C. H.: Some aspects of the introduction of modern science into China, Isis 63 (1934), 173-219.
Ch'en, K.: Matteo Ricci's contribution to and influence on geographical knowledge in China, JAOS 59 (1939), 325-359, 509.
Szczesniak, B.: Notes on the penetration of the Copernican theory into China (17th to 19th centuries), JRAS (1945), 30-38.
Bernard, H.: Notes on the introduction of the natural sciences, Yenching jo. of social studies 3 (1941), 220-241.
Duyvendak, J. J. L.: bibliographie, TP 38 (1948), 321-329.

3. American plant introductions to China

Ho, Ping-ti: The introduction of American food plants into China, American anthropologist, 57 (1955), 191-201.
Laufer (and Wilbur), The American plant migration, pt. 1: the potato, 69-79.

4. Christian missions in China

Latourette, A history of Christian missions in China, 105 to end.
Rosso, Apostolic legations to China of the eighteenth century.

XXVI

Chinese life in the Ch'ing

General reading: Latourette, The Chinese their history and culture, II, 513-721.

1. Taxation

Shaw, Democracy and finance in China, 119-152.

2. The sects or secret societies

Ward and Stirling, The Hung society, or the society of Heaven and Earth.
Favre, Les sociétés secrètes en Chine.
Brace, A. J.: Some secret societies in Szechuan, Jo. of the West China border research soc., 8 (1936), 177-180.
de Korne, The fellowship of goodness.

3. Education

Kuo, The Chinese system of public education, 64-109.
LaFargue, China's first hundred.
Peake, Nationalism and education in modern China, 1-71.
Lewis, The education of girls in China, chap. 2.
Gregg, China and educational autonomy.

4. Guilds

Niida, Noboru: The industrial and commercial guilds of Peking, Folklore studies 9 (1950), 179-206.
Morse, The guilds of China.

5. Mythology and popular religion

Maspero, The mythology of modern China, in Asiatic mythology, 252-384.
Eberhard, China's fairy tales and folk tales.
Bodde (tsl.), Annual customs and festivals in Peking.
Doré, Recherches sur les superstitions en Chine.

XXVII

Chinese life in the Ch'ing, continued

General reading: Escarra, China then and now, 79-103.

1. The village

Smith, Village life in China.
Kulp, Country life in south China, 106-134.
Fei, Peasant life in China, 95-286.
Yang, A Chinese village: Taitou, Shantung province.
Chang, The Chinese gentry: studies on their role in nineteenth-century Chinese society.

2. The family

Su, The Chinese family system, chap. 2 to end.
Kulp, *op. cit.*, 135-188.
Fei, *op. cit.*, 27-94.
Lamson, Social pathology in China, 493-588.
Hu, The common descent group in China and its functions.

3. Population

Buck, Land utilization in China, chap. 13.
Liu, Contribution à l'étude de la population chinoise.
Lamson, *op. cit.*, chap. 8.
Lowdermilk and Wickes: History of soil use in the Wu t'ai shan area, monograph of NCBRAS, 1938.
Chang, Chih-yi: China's population problem—a Chinese view, PA, 22 (1949), 339-356.

4. Medicine and medical practice

Wong and Wu, History of Chinese medicine, 105-254.
Matignon, Superstition, crime, et misère en Chine.

5. The press

Britton, The Chinese periodical press, 1800-1912.
Lin, A history of the press and public opinion in China, 1-113.
Löwenthal, R.: Western literature on Chinese journalism—a bibliography, Nankai soc. and econ. qu. 9 (1937), 1007-1066.

XXVIII

The establishment of the Republic

General reading: Li, The political history of China, 1840-1928, 245-505.

Linebarger and Hosack: The Republic . . . (1928-1946), in China, chap. 10.

1. The end of empire

Johnston, Twilight in the Forbidden City, chap. 6 to end.
Sharman, Sun Yat-sen, his life and its meaning, a critical biography.

2. China's international relations

Gale, E., International relations, the twentieth century, in China, chap. 12.
Bisson, Japan in China.
Rowe, China among the powers.
Fairbank, The United States and China, 174 to end.

3. China's border lands

Lattimore, Manchuria, cradle of conflict, chap. 12.
Lattimore, Nationalism and revolution in Mongolia.
Norins, Gateway to Asia: Sinkiang.

4. Industrial and social revolution

Smedley, A.: The social revolution, in China, chap. 11.
Shih, China enters the machine age.
Wu and Price, China rediscovers her west.
Lang, Chinese family and society.

5. The press

Lin, A history of the press and public opinion in China, 114-179.
Löwenthal, The religious periodical press in China.

6. The People's Republic

Wilbur and How, Documents on communism, nationalism and Soviet advisers in China, 1918-1927.
Compton, Mao's China: Party Reform Documents, 1942-1944.
Kirby, Contemporary China.
Schwartz, Chinese Communism and the rise of Mao.

China's potentialities and problems

General reading: Chan, Philosophies of China.
Winfield, China: the land and the people.
Wright, Mary C.: From revolution to restoration:
the transformation of ideology, FEQ 14
(1955), 515-532.

1. **Intellectual and literary revolution**

Chan, W. T.: Hu Shih and Chinese philosophy, Philosophy East and
West, 6 (1956), 3-12.
Hummel (tsl.), The autobiography of a Chinese historian.
de Francis, Nationalism and language reform in China.
Brière, Fifty years of Chinese philosophy, 1898-1950.

2. **Fiction and drama**

Wang (tsl.), Ah Q and others.
.... (tsl.), Contemporary Chinese stories.
.... (ed.), Stories of China at war.
Tchao, Le Théâtre chinois d'aujourd'hui.
Van Boven, Histoire de la littérature chinoise moderne.
Scott, The classical theatre of China.

3. **Education**

Peake, Nationalism and education in modern China, 72-157.
Freyn, Chinese education in the war.
Pott, F. L. H.: Modern education, in China (ed. by MacNair), 427-
440.
Also consult Current Background, prepared under direction of U. S.
Consulate-General, Hong Kong, 400 (July 17, 1956), 10-25.

4. **Economic conditions**

Buck, Chinese farm economy.
Shen, Agricultural resources of China.
Wang, The future development of the Chinese coal industry.
Chen, Population in modern China.
Kirby, Introduction to the economic history of China, chap. 19.

5. **Taiwan**

Riggs, Formosa under Chinese Nationalist rule.
Barclay, Colonial development and population in Taiwan.
Dept. of Information, Taiwan, ten years of progress.

ACKER, WILLIAM REYNOLDS BEAL. Some T'ang and pre-T'ang texts on Chinese painting (Leiden, 1954).

.... T'ao the hermit, sixty poems by T'ao Ch'ien (New York, 1952).

APPLETON, WILLIAM WORTHEN. A cycle of Cathay (New York, 1951).

ARLINGTON, L. C. & ACTON, H. (tsl. and ed.) Famous Chinese plays (Peiping, 1937).

BAGCHI, P. C. Le canon bouddhique en Chine (2 vols. Paris, 1927, 1938).

.... India and China, a thousand years of cultural relations (Bombay, 1950).

BALAZS, ÉTIENNE. Le traité juridique du "Souei-chou." (Leiden, 1954).

BALES, WILLIAM L. Tso Tsung-t'ang (Shanghai, 1937).

BARCLAY, GEORGE W. Colonial development and population in Taiwan (Princeton, 1954).

BERGMAN, FOLKE. Archeological researches in Sinkiang (Stockholm, 1939).

BERNARD, HENRI. La découverte de Nestoriens Mongols aux Ordos et l'histoire ancienne du Christianisme en extrême-orient (Tientsin, 1935).

BINGHAM, WOODBRIDGE. The fall of Sui and the rise of T'ang (Baltimore, 1941).

BISHOP, JOHN LYMAN. The colloquial short story in China (Cambridge, Mass., 1956).

BISSON, T. A. Japan in China (New York, 1938).

BODDE, DERK. (tsl.) Annual customs and festivals in Peking, by Tun, Li-ch'en (Peiping, 1936).

.... China's first unifier (Leiden, 1938).

.... Statesman, patriot, and general (New Haven, 1940).

BOXER, C. R. Fidalgos in the Far East, 1550-1770. Fact and Fancy in the history of Macao (The Hague, 1948).

.... South China in the sixteenth century (London, 1953).

BRETSCHNEIDER, EMIL. Mediaeval researches from eastern Asiatic sources (2 vols.; London, 1888).

BREWITT-TAYLOR, CHARLES H. San Kuo, or Romance of the Three Kingdoms (2 vols.; Shanghai, 1925).

BRIÈRE, O. Fifty years of Chinese philosophy, 1898-1950 (London, 1956).

BRITTON, ROSWELL S. The Chinese periodical press, 1800-1912 (Shanghai, 1933).

BROOMHALL, MARSHALL. Islam in China (London, 1910).

BRUCE, J. PERCY. Chu Hsi and his masters (London, 1922).

BUCK, JOHN L. Chinese farm economy (Chicago, 1930).

.... Land utilization in China (Chicago, 1937).

CANDLIN, CLARA. The herald wind (London, 1933).
---------------------------- The rapier of Lu, patriot poet of China (London, 1946).
CARTER, THOMAS F. & GOODRICH, L. C. The invention of printing in China and its spread westward (New York, 1955).
CHAN, WING-TSIT. Philosophies of China, reprinted from Twentieth Century Philosophy (New York, 1943).
CHANG, CHUNG-LI. The Chinese gentry: studies on their role in nineteenth-century Chinese society (Seattle, 1955).
CHANG, T'IEN-TSE. Sino-Portuguese trade from 1514 to 1644 (Leiden, 1934).
CHAVANNES, ÉDOUARD. (tsl.) Les mémoires historiques de Se-ma Ts'ien (5 vols.; Paris, 1895-1905).
CHEN, SHIH-HSIANG. Essay on literature: written by the third-century Chinese poet Lu Chi (Portland, Me., 1953).
CHEN, TA. Population in modern China (Chicago, 1946).
CHENG, ANDREW CHIH-YI. Hsüntzu's theory of human nature and its influence on Chinese thought (Peking, 1928).
CHI, CH'AO-TING. Key economic areas in Chinese history (London, 1936).
CHIANG, SIANG-TSEH. The Nien rebellion (Seattle, 1954).
CHIANG YEE. Chinese calligraphy (Cambridge, Mass., 1954).
CHRISTY, ARTHUR E. (ed.). The Asian legacy and American life (New York, 1945).
COEDÈS, G., Les états hindouisés d'Indochine et d'Indonésie (Paris, 1948).
COMPTON, BOYD. Mao's China: Party reform documents, 1942-1944 (Seattle, 1952).
CREEL, HERRLEE G. The birth of China (London, 1936).
---------------------------- Chinese thought from Confucius to Mao Tse-tung (Chicago, 1953).
---------------------------- Confucius, the man and the myth (New York, 1949).
---------------------------- Studies in early Chinese culture, 1st series (Baltimore, 1937).
CRESSEY, GEORGE B. China's Geographic Foundations (New York, 1934).
DANTON, GEORGE H. The cultural contacts of the United States and China (New York, 1931).
DAVIDSON, MARTHA. A list of published translations from Chinese into English, French, and German, 2 parts (Ann Arbor, 1952 and New Haven, 1957).
DAWSON, CHRISTOPHER HENRY. The Mongol mission, narratives and letters of Franciscan missionaries (New York, 1955).
DE CHARDIN, PIERRE TEILHARD. Early man in China (Peiping, 1941).
---------------------------- Fossil men (Peiping, 1943).
DE FRANCIS, JOHN FRANCIS. Nationalism and language reform in China (Princeton, 1950).

DE KORNE, JOHN C. The fellowship of goodness (Grand Rapids, 1941).

DENNETT, TYLER. Americans in Eastern Asia (New York, 1922).

DEVERIA, GABRIEL. Histoire des relations de la Chine avec l'Annam-Vietnam du XVIᵉ siècle d'aprés des documents chinois (Paris, 1880).

DORÉ, HENRI. Recherches sur les superstitions en Chine (10 vols.; Shanghai, 1913-1938).

DUBS, HOMER H. (tsl.) The history of the former Han dynasty, by Pan Ku (3 vols.; Baltimore, 1938, 1944, and 1955).

—————————— Hsüntze, the moulder of ancient Confucianism (London, 1927); The works of Hsüntze (London, 1928).

—————————— A Roman city in ancient China (London, 1957).

DUYVENDAK, JAN JULIUS L. (tsl.) The book of Lord Shang (London, 1928).

—————————— Tao te ching (London, 1954).

EBERHARD, WOLFRAM. Chinese fairy tales and folk tales (London, 1937).

—————————— A history of China (Berkeley, 1950).

—————————— Conquerors and rulers, social forces in mediaeval China (Leiden, 1952).

EDWARDS, E. D. Chinese prose literature of the T'ang period (2 vols.; London, 1937-1938).

ELISSEEFF, VADIME. (ed.) L'art de la Chine des Song (Paris, 1956).

ESCARRA, JEAN. China then and now (Peiping, 1940).

FAIRBANK, JOHN K. The United States and China (Cambridge, Mass., 1948).

—————————— (ed.) Chinese thought and institutions (Chicago, 1957).

FANG, CHIH-T'UNG. (tsl.) The chronicle of the Three Kingdoms (Cambridge, Mass., 1952).

FAVRE, B. Les sociétés secrètes en Chine (Paris, 1933).

FEI, HSIAO-TUNG. Peasant life in China (London, 1939).

FERRAND, GABRIEL. (tsl.) Voyage du marchand arabe Sulaymân en Inde et en Chine rédigé en 851 suivi de remarques par Abu Zayd Hasan (vers 916) (Paris, 1922).

FITZGERALD, CHARLES P. China (London, 1935).

—————————— The empress Wu (London, 1956).

—————————— Son of Heaven: a biography of Li Shih-min, founder of the T'ang dynasty (Cambridge, 1933).

FORKE, ALFRED. (tsl.) Lun-Hêng (2 vols.; London, 1907-1911).

FORKE, ANTON. (tsl.) Yang Chu's garden of pleasure (London, 1912).

FOX, GRACE. British admirals and Chinese pirates, 1832-1869 (London, 1940).

FRANKE, HERBERT. Geld und Wirtschaft in China unter der Mongolen-Herrschaft (Leipzig, 1949).

FRANKEL, HANS H. Catalogue of translations from the Chinese Dynastic histories for the period 220-960 (Berkeley and Los Angeles, 1957).

FREYN, HUBERT. Chinese education in the war (Shanghai, 1940).

FUCHS, WALTER. Beiträge zur Mandjurischen bibliographie und literatur (Tokyo, 1936).

———————————— The "Mongol atlas" of China by Chu Ssu-pen and the Kuang-yü-t'u (Peiping, 1946).

FUNG, YU-LAN. (tsl.) Chuang-tzu (Shanghai, 1933).

———————————— A history of Chinese philosophy, 2 vols. (trans. by Derk Bodde; Princeton, 1952, 1953).

———————————— A short history of Chinese philosophy (trans. by Bodde; New York, 1948).

———————————— The spirit of Chinese philosophy (trans. by Hughes; London, 1947).

GALE, ESSON McD. (tsl.) Discourses on salt and iron (Leiden, 1931).

GALLAGHER, LOUIS JOSEPH. (tsl.) China in the 16th century: the journals of Matthew Ricci, 1583-1610 (New York, 1953).

GALT, HOWARD SPILMAN. History of Chinese educational institutions (London, 1951).

GERNET, JACQUES. Les aspects économiques de Bouddhisme dans la société chinoise du Ve au Xe siècle (Saigon, 1956).

GIBERT, LUCIEN. Dictionnaire historique et géographique de la Mandchourie (Hongkong, 1934).

GILES, HERBERT A. Gems of Chinese literature (Shanghai, 1922).

———————————— History of Chinese literature (New York, 1901).

———————————— (tsl.) Strange stories from a Chinese studio (New York, 1925).

GILES, LIONEL. Six centuries of Tunhuang (London, 1944).

GOODRICH, L. CARRINGTON. The literary inquisition of Ch'ien-lung (Baltimore, 1935).

———————————— A short history of the Chinese people (rev. ed., New York, 1951).

———————————— & CARTER, THOMAS F. The invention of printing in China and its spread westward (New York, 1955).

GREENBIE, SYDNEY & MARJORIE B. Gold of Ophir, the China trade in the making of America (rev. ed.; New York, 1937).

GREGG, ALICE H. China and educational autonomy (Syracuse, 1946).

GROUSSET, RENÉ. The civilizations of the east (trans. by C. A. Phillips; 4 vols.; New York, 1931-1934).

———————————— L'empire des steppes (Paris, 1939).

———————————— Histoire de l'extrême-orient (Paris, 1929).

———————————— The rise and splendour of the Chinese empire (London, 1952).

GULIK, R. H. van. Hsi K'ang and his poetical essay on the lute (Tokyo, 1941).

HAIL, WILLIAM J. Tseng Kuo-fan and the Tai Ping rebellion (New Haven, 1927).

HALL, DANIEL GEORGE EDWARD. A history of south-east Asia (New York, 1955).

HENKE, FREDERICK G. The philosophy of Wang Yang-ming (Chicago, 1916).

HENTZE, C. Chinese tomb figures (London, 1928).

HERRMANN, ALBERT. Historical atlas of China (Cambridge, Mass., 1935).

HETHERINGTON, A. L. Chinese ceramic glazes (Cambridge, 1937).

HO, SHIH-CHUN. (tsl.) Jou Lin Wai Che, le roman des lettrés (Paris, 1933).

HOBSON, ROBERT L. A catalogue of Chinese pottery and porcelain in the collection of Sir Percival David (London, 1934).

.... The wares of the Ming dynasty (London, 1923).

HSIEH, PAO CHAO. The government of China (Baltimore, 1925).

HSÜ, SHU-HSI. China and her political entity (New York, 1926).

HU, HSIEN CHIN. The common descent group in China and its functions (New York, 1948).

HU, SHIH. The Chinese renaissance (Chicago, 1934).

HUANG, SIU-CHI. Lu Hsiang-shan, a twelfth century Chinese idealist philosopher (New Haven, 1944).

HUC, EVARISTE REGIS. A journey through the Chinese empire (2 vols.; London, 1859).

HUDSON, G. F. Europe and China (London, 1931).

HUGHES, E. R. The Great Learning and the Mean-in-action (London, 1942).

.... The invasion of China by the western world (New York, 1938).

.... & HUGHES, K. Religion in China (New York, 1950).

HULSEWÉ, ANTHONY FRANÇOIS PAULUS. Remnants of Han law (Leiden, 1955).

HUMMEL, ARTHUR W. (tsl.) The autobiography of a Chinese historian (Leiden, 1931).

.... (ed.) Eminent Chinese of the Ch'ing period (2 vols.; Washington, 1943-1944).

HUNG, WILLIAM. Tu Fu, China's greatest poet (Cambridge, Mass., 1952).

HURVITZ, LEON. Wei Shou: Treatise on Buddhism and Taoism, in Yün-kang XVI (Kyoto, 1956).

IRWIN, RICHARD GREGG. The evolution of a Chinese novel: Shui-hu-chuan (Cambridge, Mass., 1953).

ITO, CHUTA. Architectural decoration in China (trans. by Jiro Harada; 3 vols.; Tokyo, 1941-1942).

JANSÉ, OLOV. Archeological research in Indo-China (Cambridge, Mass., 1947).

.... Briques et objets céramiques funéraires de l'époque des Han (Paris, 1936).

JOHNSTON, REGINALD F. Twilight in the Forbidden City (New York, 1934).

KAMMERER, ALBERT. La découverte de la Chine par les Portugais au XVIe siècle (Leiden, 1944).

KAO, GEORGE. (ed.) Chinese wit and humor (New York, 1946).

KARLGREN, BERNHARD. The Chinese language (New York, 1949).

.... The book of Odes (Stockholm, 1950).

KIRBY, E. STUART. (ed.) Contemporary China. (Hongkong, 1956).

.... Introduction to the economic history of China (London, 1954).

KOU, PAO-KOH. Deux sophistes chinois, Houei et Kong-souen Long (Paris, 1953).

KRACKE, EDWARD A. Civil service in early Sung China (Cambridge, Mass., 1953).

KRAMERS, R. P. K'ung tzu chia yü, the school sayings of Confucius (Leiden, 1950).

KULP, DANIEL H. Country life in south China (New York, 1925).

KUNO, YOSHI SABURO. Japanese expansion on the Asiatic continent (2 vols.; Berkeley, 1937-1940).

KUO, PIN CHIA. A critical study of the first Anglo-Chinese war, with documents (Shanghai, 1935).

KUO, PING WEN. The Chinese system of public education (New York, 1914).

LA FARGUE, THOMAS. China's first hundred (Pullman, 1942).

LACH, DONALD F. Contributions of China to German civilization, 1648-1740 (Chicago, 1944).

LAMSON, HERBERT D. Social pathology in China (Shanghai, 1935).

LANG, OLGA. Chinese family and society (New Haven, 1946).

LANGER, W. L. (ed.) An Encyclopaedia of World History (Boston, 1940).

LATOURETTE, KENNETH S. The Chinese their history and culture (3rd ed., rev.; 2 vols.; New York, 1956).

.... A history of Christian missions in China (New York, 1929).

LATTIMORE, OWEN. Inner Asian frontiers of China (New York, 1951).

.... Manchuria, cradle of conflict (New York, 1932).

.... Nationalism and revolution in Mongolia (New York, 1955).

LAUFER, BERTHOLD. The American plant migration, pt. 1: the potato (prepared for publication by C. Martin Wilbur; Chicago, 1938).

.... The beginnings of porcelain in China (Chicago, 1917).

.... Chinese pottery of the Han dynasty (Leiden, 1909).

.... Sino-Iranica (Chicago, 1919).

LEGGE, JAMES. Chinese classics (5 vols., 2nd ed.; Oxford, 1893-1895).

LEVIS, JOHN H. Foundations of Chinese musical art (Peking, 1936).

51

LEVY, HOWARD S. Biography of Huang Ch'ao (Berkeley, 1955).

LEWIS, IDA BELLE. The education of girls in China (New York, 1919).

LI, CHI. The beginnings of Chinese civilization (Seattle, 1957).

————————————— (ed.) Ch'êng-tzŭ-yai, the black pottery culture site (New Haven, 1956).

LI, CHIEN-NUNG. The political history of China, 1840-1928 (Princeton, 1956).

LI, CHOU CHUNG-CHENG. L'examen provincial en Chine . . . sous la dynastie des Ts'ing (Paris, 1935).

LI, HSIUNG-FEI. Les censeurs sous la dynastie mandchoue (1616-1911) en Chine (Paris, 1936).

LI, TIEH-TSENG. The historical status of Tibet (New York, 1956).

LIAO, WEN-KUEI. (tsl.) Han Fei Tzu (London, 1939).

LIM, BOON KENG. (tsl.) The Li Sao, an elegy on encountering sorrows, by Ch'ü Yüan (Shanghai, 1929).

LIN, MOUSHENG. Men and ideas, an informal history of Chinese political thought (New York, 1942).

LIN, YUTANG. The gay genius: the life and times of Su Tungpo (New York, 1947).

————————————— A history of the press and public opinion in China (Shanghai, 1936).

————————————— (tsl.) The nun of T'ai-shan (Shanghai, 1936).

LIU, NAN-MING. Contributions à l'étude de la population chinoise (Geneva, 1935).

LIU, WU-CHI. A short history of Confucian philosophy (Harmondsworth, Middlesex, Eng., 1955).

LOEHR, MAX. Chinese bronze age weapons (Ann Arbor, 1956).

LÖWENTHAL, RUDOLF. The religious periodical press in China (Peiping, 1940).

LU, LIEN-TCHING. Les greniers publics de prévoyance sous la dynastie des Ts'ing (Paris, 1932).

LYALL, LEONARD A. (tsl.) Mencius (London, 1932).

MacNAIR, HARLEY F. (ed.) China (Berkeley and Los Angeles, 1946).

MALONE, CARROLL B. History of the Peking summer palaces under the Ch'ing dynasty (Urbana, 1934).

MARGOULIES, GEORGES. Anthologie raisonnée de la littérature chinoise (Paris, 1948).

————————————— Le Kou-wen chinois (Paris, 1926).

MARTIN, HENRY DESMOND. The rise of Chinghis Khan and his conquest of North China (Baltimore, 1950).

MASPERO, HENRI. La Chine antique (Paris, 1927).

————————————— Les documents chinois de la troisième expedition de Sir Aurel Stein en Asie centrale (London, 1953).

————————————— Mélanges posthumes (3 vols., Paris, 1950).

MATIGNON, JEAN J. Superstition, crime, et misère en Chine (Paris, 1936).

MAVERICK, LEWIS ADAMS. China, a model for Europe (San Antonio, 1941).

.... (ed.) Economic dialogues in ancient China, selections from the Kuan-tzu (Carbondale, Ill., 1954).

MEI, YI-PAO. (tsl.) The ethical and political works of Motse (London, 1929).

.... Motse, the neglected rival of Confucius (London, 1934).

MICHAEL, FRANZ. The origin of Manchu rule in China (Baltimore, 1942).

MIKAMI, Y. The development of mathematics in China and Japan (Leipzig, 1913).

MINORSKY, V. Marvazi on China, the Turks and India (London, 1942).

MORSE, HOSEA B. The chronicles of the East India Company trading to China (5 vols.; Oxford, 1926-1929).

.... The guilds of China (2nd ed.; London, 1932).

.... & MacNAIR, H. F. Far Eastern international relations (Boston, 1931).

MOULE, ARTHUR C. Christians in China: before the year 1550 (New York, 1930).

.... Nestorians in China (London, 1940).

.... Quinsai, with other notes on Marco Polo (Cambridge, 1957).

.... The rulers of China, 221 B.C.–A.D. 1949 (London, 1957).

.... & PELLIOT, PAUL. Marco Polo, the description of the world (2 vols.; London, 1938).

NEEDHAM, JOSEPH & WANG, LING. Science and civilization in China, 1956 (Cambridge, 1954, 2 vols.).

NORINS, MARTIN R. Gateway to Asia: Sinkiang (New York, 1944).

OLSCHKI, LEONARDO. Guillaume Boucher, a French artist at the Court of the Khans (Baltimore, 1946).

.... Marco Polo's precursors (Baltimore, 1943).

OU, ITAI. Essai critique et bibliographique sur le roman chinois (Paris, 1933).

PAVLOVSKY, MICHEL N. Chinese-Russian relations (New York, 1949).

PEAKE, CYRUS H. Nationalism and education in modern China (New York, 1932).

PELLIOT, PAUL. Mémoires sur les coutumes du Cambodge de Tcheou Ta-kuan, version nouvelle (Paris, 1951).

PETECH, LUCIANO. China and Tibet in the early 18th century (Leiden, 1950).

POKOTILOV, D. History of the eastern Mongols during the Ming dynasty from 1368 to 1634 (trans. by Löwenthal, Chengtu, 1947).

POPE, JOHN ALEXANDER. Chinese porcelains from the Ardebil shrine (Washington, 1956).

POUZYNA, I. V. La Chine, l'Italie et les débuts de la Renaissance (XIIIᵉ-XIVᵉ siècles) (Paris, 1935).

PRIP-MØLLER, JOHANNES. Chinese Buddhist monasteries (London, 1937).

PULLEYBLANK, E. G. The background of the rebellion of An Lu-shan (Oxford, 1955).

REICHWEIN, ADOLF. China and Europe (trans. by J. C. Powell; New York, 1925).

REISCHAUER, EDWIN O. Ennin's Travels in T'ang China (New York, 1955).

.... (tsl.) Ennin's Diary (New York, 1955).

RIGGS, FREDERICK WARREN. Formosa under Chinese Nationalist rule (New York, 1952).

ROCKHILL, WILLIAM W. China's intercourse with Korea from the XVth century to 1895 (London, 1905).

ROSSO, ANTONIO SISTO. Apostolic Legations to China of the eighteenth century (South Pasadena, 1948).

ROTOURS, ROBERT des. (tsl.) Le traité des examens traduit de la Nouvelle Histoire des T'ang (Paris, 1932).

.... Traité des fonctionnaires et traité de l'armée, traduits de la Nouvelle Histoire des T'ang (2 vols.; Leiden, 1947-1948).

ROWBOTHAM, ARNOLD H. Missionary and mandarin, the Jesuits at the court of China (Berkeley and Los Angeles, 1942).

ROWE, DAVID NELSON. China among the powers (New York, 1945).

RUDOLPH, RICHARD C. Han tomb art of West China (Berkeley, Calif., 1951).

SACHS, CURT. The rise of music in the ancient world, east and west (New York, 1943).

SAEKI, P. YOSHIO. Nestorian documents and relics in China (Tokyo, 1937).

SAKANISHI, SHIO. (tsl.) An essay on landscape painting by Kuo Hsi (London, 1935).

SANSOM, SIR GEORGE B. Japan, a short cultural history (rev. ed.; New York, 1943).

SAUVAGET, JEAN. (tsl.) Relation de le Chine et de l'Inde (Paris, 1948).

SCHAFER, EDWARD H. The empire of Min (Rutland, Vt., 1954).

.... The history of the empire of Southern Han, in Silver Jubilee Vol. . . . of Kyoto Univ. (Kyoto, 1954).

SCHURMANN, HERBERT FRANZ. (tsl.) Economic structure of the Yüan dynasty (Cambridge, Mass., 1956).

SCHURZ, WILLIAM L. The Manila galleon (New York, 1939).

SCHWARTZ, BENJAMIN I. Chinese Communism and the rise of Mao (Cambridge, Mass., 1951).

SCOTT, A. C. The classical theatre of China (New York, 1957).

SEKINO, TADASHI & TAKESHIMA, TAKUICHI. Jehol (4 vols.; Tokyo, 1934).

SERRUYS, HENRY. Sino-Jürčed relations during the Yung-lo period (Wiesbaden, Ger., 1955).

SHABAD, THEODORE. China's changing map (New York, 1956).

SHARMAN, LYON. Sun Yat-sen, his life and its meaning, a critical biography (New York, 1934).

SHAW, KINN-WEI. Democracy and finance in China (New York, 1926).

SHEN, TSUNG-HAN. Agricultural resources of China (Ithaca, 1951).

SHIH, KUO-HENG. China enters the machine age (trans. by Fei and Hsü; Cambridge, Mass., 1944).

SHRYOCK, JOHN K. The origin and development of the state cult of Confucius (New York, 1932).

.... The study of human abilities. The Jen wu chih of Liu Shao (New Haven, 1937).

SICKMAN, LAURENCE & SOPER, ALEXANDER. The art and architecture of China (Harmondsworth, Middlesex, Eng., 1956).

SILVER JUBILEE VOLUME OF THE ZINBUN-KAGAKU-KEN-KYUSYO, KYOTO UNIVERSITY (Kyoto, 1954).

SIRÉN, OSVALD. Chinese sculpture from the 5th to 14th centuries (Paris, 1926).

.... Gardens of China (New York, 1949).

.... A history of early Chinese painting (2 vols.; London, 1933).

.... A history of later Chinese painting (2 vols.; London, 1938).

SMITH, ARTHUR H. Village life in China (4th ed.; New York, 1899).

SOPER, ALEXANDER COBURN. Kuo Jo-hsü's experiences in painting (Washington, 1951).

STAUNTON, GEORGE T. Ta Tsing Leu Lee (London, 1810).

STEIN, SIR MARK AUREL. On ancient Central-Asian tracks (London, 1933).

SU, SING GING. The Chinese family system (New York, 1922).

SUN, I-TU JEN. Chinese railways and British interests, 1898-1911 (New York, 1954).

SWANN, NANCY LEE. Pan Chao, the foremost woman scholar of China (New York, 1932).

.... Food & money in ancient China, Han shu 24 (Princeton, 1950).

SWISHER, EARL. China's management of the American barbarians (New Haven, 1953).

TAIWAN DEPT. OF INFORMATION. Taiwan, ten years of progress (Taipei, 1956).

TAN, CH'UN-LIN CHESTER. The Boxer catastrophe (New York, 1955).

TCHIAO, T. T. Le théâtre chinois d'aujourd'hui (Paris, 1938).

TEGGART, FREDERICK J. Rome and China (Berkeley, 1939).

55

TENG, SSU-YU. Chang Hsi and the treaty of Nanking, 1842 (Chicago, 1944).

.... & FAIRBANK, J. K. China's response to the West (Cambridge, Mass., 1954).

TJAN, TJOE SOM. Po hu t'ung. The comprehensive discussions in the White Tiger Hall (Leiden, 1949).

TOBAR, J. Inscriptions juives de K'ai-fong-fou (Shanghai, 1900).

TORII, RYUZO. Sculptured stone tombs of the Liao dynasty (Peking, 1942).

TREVER, CAMILLA. Excavations in northern Mongolia (1924-1925) (Leningrad, 1932).

TSUNODA, RYUSAKU. Japan in the Chinese dynastic histories (South Pasadena, Calif., 1951).

VAN BOVEN, HENRI. Histoire de la littérature chinois moderne (Peiping, 1946).

WALEY, ARTHUR. (tsl.) The analects of Confucius (London, 1938).

.... (tsl.) The book of songs (London, 1937).

.... (tsl.) Ch'ang-ch'un, the travels of an alchemist (London, 1931).

.... (tsl.) An introduction to the study of Chinese painting (London, 1923).

.... The life and times of Po Chü-i (London, 1949).

.... (tsl.) The Nine Songs (New York, 1956).

.... The poetry and career of Li Po, 701-762 (New York, 1950).

.... The real Tripitaka (London, 1952).

.... (tsl.) Three ways of thought in ancient China (London, 1939).

.... Yuan Mei, eighteenth century Chinese poet (London, 1956).

.... (tsl.) Translations from the Chinese (New York, 1941).

.... (tsl.) The Way and its power (London, 1934).

WANG, CHI-CHEN. (tsl.) Ah Q and others (New York, 1941).

.... (tsl.) Contemporary Chinese stories (New York, 1944).

.... (tsl.) Dream of the red chamber, by Tsao Hsüeh-chin and Kao Ngoh (New York, 1958).

.... (ed.) Stories of China at war (New York, 1947).

.... (tsl.) Traditional Chinese tales (New York, 1944).

WANG, KUNG-PING. The future development of the Chinese coal industry (New York, 1947).

WANG, TCH'ANG-TCHE. La philosophie morale de Wang Yang-ming (Shanghai, 1936).

WANG, YI-T'UNG. Official relations between China and Japan, 1368-1549 (Cambridge, Mass., 1953).

WANG, YU-CHUAN. Early Chinese coinage (New York, 1951).

WARD, JOHN S. M. & STIRLING, WILLIAM G. The Hung society or the society of Heaven and Earth (3 vols.; London, 1925-1926).

WEI, FRANCIS C. M. The spirit of Chinese culture (New York, 1947).

WELCH, HOLMES. The parting of the way: Lao Tzu and the Taoist movement (Boston, 1957).

WENLEY, A. G. et al. A descriptive and illustrative catalogue of Chinese bronzes (Washington, 1946).

WHITE, WILLIAM C. Chinese Jews (3 pts.; Toronto, 1942).

----------------------------- Tomb tile pictures of ancient China (Toronto, 1939).

----------------------------- Tombs of old Lo-yang (Shanghai, 1934).

WILBUR, C. MARTIN. Slavery in China during the former Han dynasty (Chicago, 1943).

----------------------------- & HOW, JULIE LIEN-YING. Documents on communism, nationalism and Soviet advisers in China, 1918-1927 (New York, 1956).

WILLIAMSON, HENRY R. Wang An Shih (2 vols.; London, 1935-1937).

WINFIELD, GERALD. China: the land and the people (New York, 1948).

WITTFOGEL, KARL A. Oriental despotism (New Haven, 1957).

----------------------------- & FENG, CHIA-SHENG. History of Chinese society, Liao (907-1125) (New York, 1949).

WONG, K. CHIMIN & WU, LIEN-TEH. History of Chinese medicine (Tientsin, 1932).

WRIGHT, MARY C. The last stand of Chinese conservatism, the T'ung-chih restoration, 1862-1874 (Stanford, 1957).

WU, YI-FANG & PRICE, F. W. China rediscovers her west (London, 1942).

YANG, MARTIN C. A Chinese village. Taitou, Shantung province (New York, 1945).

ZI, ETIENNE. Pratique des examens littéraires en Chine (Shanghai, 1894).

ZUCKER, ADOLPH E. The Chinese theater (Boston, 1925).

PERIODICALS

Only those periodicals mentioned in the text which are more or less concerned with China and Chinese studies are listed below.

Name	Abbreviation
Artibus Asiae, Ascona	
Asia Major, Leipzig and London	AM
Bulletin de l'Ecole Française d'Extrême Orient, Hanoi and Saigon	BEFEO
Bulletin of the Museum of Far Eastern Antiquities, Stockholm	BMFEA
Bulletin of the School of Oriental (and African) Studies, London	BSO(A)S
Chinese Social and Political Science Review, Peking	CSPSR
Etudes Asiatiques, Berne	
Far Eastern Quarterly (up to 1956), Ann Arbor	FEQ
Harvard Journal of Asiatic Studies, Cambridge	HJAS
Journal Asiatique, Paris	JA
Journal of Asian Studies (since Nov. 1956), Ann Arbor	JAS
Journal of the American Oriental Society, New Haven	JAOS
Journal of the Royal Asiatic Society, London	JRAS
Journal of the Royal Asiatic Society—(North) China Branch, Shanghai	J(N)CBRAS
Mélanges Chinois et Bouddhiques, Brussels	MCB
Memoirs of the Research Department of the Toyo Bunko, Tokyo	MTB
Monumenta Serica, Peking and Tokyo	MS
Pacific Affairs, Richmond, Va.	PA
Revue des Arts Asiatiques, Paris	RAA
T'ien Hsia Monthly, Shanghai and Hong Kong	THM
T'oung Pao, Leiden	TP

APPENDIX

1. Physical and political geography

It is well for anyone attempting the study of China's past to become acquainted first of all with the map of China, and learn the names of the important rivers and mountain ranges from the Pamirs and the Ili east to the Yellow Sea; the names too of the provinces and the chief cities; and the resources of each area. A brief description of the physical character-istics of China is given by Kenneth Scott Latourette in *The Chinese Their History and Culture*, I, chapter 1. For a fuller study of "the land and its people" see George B. Cressey, *China's Geographic Foundations*. A useful supplement for historical studies is Albert Herrmann, *Historical Atlas of China*, and for the recent past Theodore Shabad, *China's Changing Map: a political and economic geography of the Chinese People's Republic*.

2. Bibliography

Those who wish to build up a select library of Western books on China or who desire to consult reviews of many of the works cited above are referred to Charles S. Gardner, *A Union List of Selected Western Books on China in American Libraries*, second ed., revised and enlarged, published by the American Council of Learned Societies, Washington, D. C. (1938). To this should be added: Richard L. Walker, *Western Language Period-icals on China (a selective list)*, published by the Institute of Far Eastern Languages, Yale University, New Haven, Conn. (1949). Another work which lists both books and articles appearing in many languages, including Chinese, Japanese, and Russian, is Robert J. Kerner, *Northeastern Asia, a Selected Bibliography*, 2 vols. (1939). For current bibliography consult the *Journal of Oriental Studies, Monumenta Serica*, and *Far Eastern Quarterly*, since November 1956 entitled the *Journal of Asian Studies*. For lists of translations into European languages consult Martha Davidson, *A list of published translations from Chinese*, parts I and II, and Hans H. Frankel, *Catalogue of translations from the Chinese dynastic histories for the period 220-960*.

3. Dates

For a concise chronological treatment of important events in Chinese history, see W. L. Langer (ed.), *An Encyclopaedia of World History*, and A. C. Moule, *The Rulers of China, 221 B.C.–A.D. 1949*.

NOTES

NOTES

NOTES

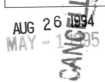